the Book of appearing & disappearing

tHE BOOK OF aPPeaRiNG & DisaPPeaRiNG

by Tom Mason and Dan Danko
with John Railing and Danny Orleans, Professional Magicians

Scholastic Inc.
New York • Toronto • London • Auckland • Sydney
Mexico City • New Delhi • Hong Kong • Buenos Aires

ISBN 0-439-32704-0

Copyright © 2001 by Scholastic Inc.

Design by Mark Neston
Illustrations by Daniel Aycock

12 11 10 9 8 7 6 5 4 3 2 1   1 2 3 4 5 6/0

Printed in the U.S.A.

First Scholastic printing, December 2001

tABLE of CONTENTS

mirror, mirror on the wall, is my magic the best of all?

Performing magic is never easy. Once you learn a trick and perform it for your friends and family, you'll often hear them say, "*I know how that works. It's done with mirrors!*"

What do they mean by that? Well, lots of times, magicians have mirrors built into a magic box to hide something with which they want to surprise their audience, such as a hand-kerchief, some money, or a beautiful assistant. The magician then seemingly pulls the object out of thin air! We're not going to teach you that right now. But what we *will* show you is that a large part of magic *is* done with mirrors, if not exactly in the way that your audience thinks it is. This month, you'll learn the secrets of mirrors and how they can help you master your magic. Here's a hint: Mirrors are the perfect audience for your practice. And it's not just because they can't interrupt, talk back, ask questions, or pretend that they're know-it-alls!

This month Magic U. will teach you the secrets that make silk handkerchiefs, money, knots, and sponge balls appear and disappear right before the very amazed eyes of your audience. No, really. We'll teach, you'll learn, and things will appear and disappear, just like that! (Wait till you discover the secret flap in **Beam It Up!** Or the hidden compartment in **The Black Hole**.)

When you practice this month's tricks, especially **Spongy Jumping** and **Knot It!**, watch yourself in a mirror so you can see what your audience will see—and help yourself improve the way you handle your props.

Watching yourself in the mirror isn't about just making sure your hair isn't sticking out somewhere or that you don't have something stuck between your teeth! It's for improving your sleight-of-hand techniques. When you do the **French Drop**, do you properly hide the coin in your left hand? When you perform **Poof!** will your audience see where everything went? Your practice mirror has the answer.

Practice is the repetition of the hand movements with props (coins, boxes, rope, balls, you-name-its). The idea is to do them over and over until you can do them easily and smoothly and without watching your hands.

Rehearsal comes after you have practiced the individual moves and sleights—and no longer need the mirror. When you rehearse, you combine the moves with all your patter, from start to finish, exactly as you'd do the tricks in front of an audience.

Don't stop if you make a mistake. All magicians make mistakes. They drop balls, put coins in the wrong hands, and forget how to tie a knot. That's all part of learning. Just keep going—bulldog your way through it. That's how you'll teach yourself to go from beginning to end and complete a routine.

So let's review: *Practice* in front of a mirror, but *rehearse* without one. The mirror won't be there when you perform the routine, so don't get used to it. And remember:

PRACTICE + REHEARSAL = GREAT MAGIC.

And great magic is what'll amaze your friends, family, and whoever else is in your audience!

—Tom Mason and Dan Danko

the tricks

Beam it up! #1

assignment:
Make a card disappear from the Magic Card Case and reappear in your pocket!

Beam it up!
This trick is great because it uses two identical cards—one card is hidden in your pocket, and the other is hidden in the Magic Card Case, behind a removable flap that acts as a false back. When you're done, the audience thinks the card has moved from the Magic Card Case to your pocket!

magic must-haves: Magic trunk

from your appearing and disappearing kit: Magic Card Case

Homemade magic:
Two decks of cards with matching backs, although you really only need one card from the second deck; small flashlight (optional)

extras: A volunteer who doesn't know the trick

Backstage
Sort through the first deck, and pull out a random card—we'll use the four of clubs as our example. Place it on top of the first deck, facedown like the other cards. Now go through the second deck, and take out the four of clubs. Congratulations, you've got twins! Put this second four of clubs in your right pocket. Hide the second deck somewhere backstage—it's dismissed!—and place the first deck down on the magic trunk.

> **Trick Tip:** You don't have to use playing cards for this trick. You can substitute two identical pieces of paper—as long as they can fit into the Magic Card Case!

show time!
"Here's a question. Can playing cards travel through space without getting airsick?"

STEP 1: Call up a volunteer from the audience.

"Cut the deck, and we'll find out."

STEP 2: Your volunteer should cut the deck so that there are two distinct piles on the magic trunk. Don't let him put the deck back together or you'll lose track of the four of clubs. If you've been practicing the *cross cut force* that you used last month in *The Book of Mentalism* for the **Ball Gazer** trick, you already know what's going to happen. You're going to force your volunteer to choose the card you want him to. Sweet! (If you've lost track of this technique, not to worry—check out steps 3–7.)

"Great, let's mark your cut..."

STEP 3: Now, here's the tricky part. Pick up what used to be the bottom portion of the deck (stack B),

A

B

and place it sideways on top of what used to be the top portion of the deck (stack A).

"...like so."

STEP 4: Pull out the Magic Card Case and set it next to the stack of cards.

"This is my magic teleportation box."

STEP 5: Open the box, and show the inside.

"It's black on the outside, black on the inside, and completely empty."

HIDDEN FLAP

STEP 6: Remove stack B from stack A.

"Let's take the card that you cut to."

STEP 7: Now turn over the card that's on top of stack A. If you've been paying attention, then you already know that this is the four of clubs—the top card on the deck when you started!

MAGICIAN'S VIEW

"Ahhh. The four of clubs...let's put that in the teleportation chamber."

STEP 8: Take the four of clubs, and place it in the half of the Magic Card Case that is nearest to you. The hidden flap should be in the other half of the Magic Card Case.

"Okay, we're ready to teleport."

STEP 9: Close the Magic Card Case by bringing the lid farthest away from you toward you—this brings the hidden flap over to cover up the four of clubs inside.

"Beam it up!"

STEP 10: If you're good at sound effects (and who isn't?), do your best imitation of the sound of a transporter beam—like the one they use on *Star Trek*, for example. You could even shine a flashlight at the Magic Card Case and then point the beam at your pocket if you want to.

"That should do it."

STEP 11: Open the case and peek in, but don't let your audience see.

"Let's take a look."

STEP 12: Open the Magic Card Case by lifting the same lid of the case that you used to close it—the flap has covered up your four of clubs, and it looks like the case is empty. Show the case to the audience.

"Well, at least it disappeared from the transporter. I wonder where it went.... Wait, I feel something."

STEP 13: Jiggle your right leg a bit, like something's tickling you.

"Yes, I can feel it."

STEP 14: Reach into your pocket, and remove the duplicate four of clubs that you hid there.

"The teleportation is complete. Here is your card!"

STEP 15: Show the face of the card to your audience, and take a bow.

HOMEWORK:

The manipulation of the Magic Card Case is everything in this trick. Work it, love it, become its best friend so that you are totally at ease with opening it and closing it the right way.

see the SHRINK

assignment: Shrink a playing card, and then restore it to its original size!

card reduction
The Magic Card Case has a special interior flap that alternately hides the smaller card and the normal card.

magic must-haves: Magic trunk

from your appearing and disappearing kit: Magic Card Case, miniature card

Homemade magic:
A regular playing card of the same suit and value as the miniature card

Backstage
Place the miniature card facedown in the Magic Card Case. Cover the card with the flap. Now you're ready to go!

show time!
"Did you ever wonder where cards come from?"

STEP 1: Hold out the open case to the audience. The half of the case with the miniature card (hidden by the flap) should be pointing toward the audience. The other half of the case should also be empty and facing you.

MAGICIAN'S VIEW

"I used to think they just printed them in giant factories."

STEP 2: Take the regular playing card, and place it faceup inside the half of the case without the flap. The flap should still be covering your miniature card.

"But it turns out I was wrong."

STEP 3: Close the case. This is the tricky part; you've got to close the case by bringing the half hiding the miniature card toward you.

"It so happens that cards..."

STEP 4: Wave your hand over the case.

"...are a lot like people."

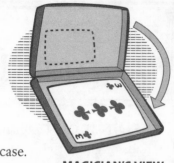

MAGICIAN'S VIEW

STEP 5: Open the lid that you just closed. You'll be opening it toward your audience (or away from you). When you do, the flap will be covering the normal-sized card and the miniature card will be resting on the flap. The mini card will be faceup. Let them take a good long look—this'll be as close as many of them ever get to a tiny card!

"They start out very, very small. Just like babies."

STEP 6: Now you're going to close the case by bringing the half of the case closest to you over to the half of the case facing the audience. This causes the flap to flip over to the other side of the case, covering the tiny card.

"But if you take care of them, feed them the right kinds of food, send them to good card schools, and give them plenty of exercise..."

STEP 7: Wave your hand over the case (in the reverse direction you waved it before). Open the box by raising the lid toward you (the same lid you used to close the case). Voilà! The audience now sees the back of the normal-size playing card!

"...they grow up to be big, strong playing cards!"

STEP 8: Take out the card from the case and close the box. Turn the card over and show the audience that it's the same card you started with!

> **Trick Tip 1:** Wouldn't this be an even cooler trick if you were shrinking a card that someone from the audience had picked from your deck? You bet it would! Here's where your past Magic U. knowledge can pay off big! Use the *cross cut force* from **Trick #1: Beam It Up!** to get a volunteer to choose the card that matches your miniature card!

> **Trick Tip 2:** Sometimes the flap gets stuck in the Magic Card Case, and won't lie flat inside the case. If you tap the case a few times before you open it, the flap should get unstuck.

HOMEWORK: I'll bet you never thought that opening and closing a box could be so crucial to a magic trick! Practice opening and closing the Magic Card Case so that the flap falls the way you want it and hides the correct card at the right time!

CASE HISTORY

Magic card cases have been around for a while. The British magician Lane had a gimmicked card case similar to yours way back in 1788. To avoid having it look suspicious, magicians often disguise *their* card cases as everyday items like business card holders, cigarette cases, wallets, and videocassette boxes!

CaRD CutteR #3

assignment: Cut a card into pieces, and then restore it!

the caRd doctoR

This is another great Magic Card Case trick that's a slight variation on the first two. There are two duplicate cards—one is hidden in the case behind the flap, and the other is cut into pieces and placed in the empty half of the case. When the case is opened, the card is "restored"!

magic must-haves: Magic trunk

from your appearing and disappearing kit: Magic Card Case

Homemade magic: A pair of scissors and two decks of playing cards with identical backs. You're going to be totally destroying one of the decks, so be prepared!

extras: A volunteer who doesn't know the trick

> **Trick Tip:** If you use playing cards for this trick, you can perform it fifty-two times using one extra deck of cards (which will be absolutely shredded when you're done, as we said). If you don't want to go around cutting up cards like some crazy card butcher, relax. There is an alternative! Just use two identical pieces of paper—same color and size—or even two identical photographs!

backstage

Sort through your first deck, and pull out a random card. Let's use the eight of diamonds this time. Place the eight of diamonds on top of the first deck. Go through the second deck, and pull out its eight of diamonds. Place this duplicate one inside the Magic Card Case—facedown, under the flap. The opened case should look like there's nothing inside. Toss the second deck off to the side—you don't need it anymore. Place the first deck facedown on the magic trunk. If you want to add a little joke at the end of this trick, write down "**One Card Surgery: $10,000**" on a piece of paper, and slip it into your pocket.

SHOW time!

"There have been a number of advances in medical science, but none of them is as amazing as card repair."

STEP 1: Call up a volunteer from the audience.

"Cut the deck, and I'll show you."

STEP 2: Your volunteer should cut the deck so that there are two piles, side by side on the magic trunk. You guessed it—it's time for the *cross cut force* again!

"Great! Let's mark your cut right here..."

STEP 3: Now it's time for the force to be with you! Pick up what used to be the bottom portion of the deck (stack B), and place it sideways on top of what used to be the top portion of the deck (stack A).

"...like so."

STEP 4: Open up the Magic Card Case, and let the audience see that it's empty. The half hiding the eight of diamonds should be facing the audience and the other empty half of the case should be facing you.

"This is the hospital where all the surgery takes place."

STEP 5: Remove stack B from stack A. You're back where you started, but the audience won't know it, if you misdirected them successfully. If you didn't, now's the time for a quick exit.

"All we need is a patient, so let's look at the card you cut to."

STEP 6: Pick up the card off the top of stack A. It's the eight of diamonds (as if you didn't already know).

"Ahhh...the eight of diamonds."

STEP 7: Hand the eight of diamonds and the scissors to your volunteer.

"Now, I want you to cut this card into four pieces. Don't worry, cards don't feel pain."

(As he cuts the card, feel free to let out a small scream, and then say, **"Sorry, it just *looks* like it's hurting the card."**)

STEP 8: After he cuts the card into four pieces, place those pieces inside the empty compartment of the Magic Card Case. Close the case by bringing the lid (which is hiding the intact card) facing the audience toward you.

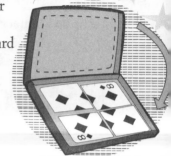

"The patient has been admitted to the hospital. Let the healing begin!"

STEP 9: Make a magic gesture—a snap of the fingers, a wave of the hand or your magic wand, or just blow on the Magic Card Case (or ask someone in the audience to do it for you).

"Now, let's see how our patient did."

STEP 10: Open the Magic Card Case, using the same lid you used to close the case. The card pieces are magically restored!

"And the operation is a success! The patient has been healed—without stitches and without a scar."

STEP 11: Remember that piece of paper in your pocket? Take it out, and hand it to your volunteer.

"And here is your hospital bill!"

HOMEWORK: It's pretty much the same homework assignment as the other two Magic Card Case tricks—you've got to be able to handle the case with natural hand movements. If you start fumbling around with it or have trouble opening and closing it, your audience is going to suspect! And we can't have that!

assignment: Pull a handkerchief from an empty cardboard box!

where's my hanky?

It's right in the box, just where you left it! That's the funny thing about secret compartments—they're always hiding stuff from the audience!

from your appearing and disappearing kit: The Black Box, two blue handkerchiefs, and assorted magic props (see BACKSTAGE)

backstage

Assemble the Black Box. Here's how. There's a piece on one long side that fits into a slot on the other long side. Then fold the bottom flap (check

TOP

Side slot

Side piece

Bottom flap

> **Trick Tip:** If you can fit it into the secret compartment, you can "produce" it from thin air. Experiment with rope, string, scarves, cards, ribbon, a banner that says Happy Birthday, your dad's old necktie, even an old sock (make it a clean one, though)!

the picture to see which end's the bottom) inside the box. If you look inside the box, you'll see a sort of pocket inside along one of the long walls—that's the secret compartment! Take one of the handkerchiefs and hide it inside the secret compartment. Just stuff it right in there so no one can see it. Then take a few of your magic props—a die, the Magic Card Case, a playing card, a sponge ball, etc.—and put them inside the box.

show time!

"I got this box for my birthday."

Hidden compartment

STEP 1: Hold up the box for the audience to see.

"It's kind of a lame gift from my wacky Uncle Charley."

STEP 2: Start taking things out of the box, one at a time, but leave in the sponge ball.

"I keep some of my magic supplies in there. My lucky die, my favorite playing card…"

STEP 3: When only the sponge ball remains inside, turn the box upside down, and let the ball bounce out.

"…but I can never seem to find my magic handkerchief."

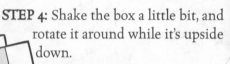

STEP 4: Shake the box a little bit, and rotate it around while it's upside down.

"That's when my wacky Uncle Charley told me that it's really not a box, it's a black hole in disguise."

STEP 5: Shake the box harder. Nothing comes out.

"I asked him what that meant."

STEP 6: Now, cover the secret compartment with one hand while you take the box apart with the other. Show the inside of the box to the audience, and pretend to be confused. (As you show the box, keep hiding the secret compartment with your hand—otherwise, it's the not-so-secret compartment!)

"And he said that the box is bigger than it seems."

STEP 7: Reassemble the box, and as you turn the box right side up, turn it so that the secret compartment is on the side farthest from the audience. (This also means that it's closest to you!)

"So my magic handkerchief must be in here somewhere."

STEP 8: Reach into the box, and really look like you're feeling around. Then, before everyone in the audience gets bored, pull out the handkerchief from the secret compartment. (Be sure to hold the box vertically so your audience can't see where the scarf was really hidden.)

"Ahhhh. Here it is!"

HOMEWORK: Practice taking apart the box and reassembling it in front of a mirror. You need to be able to do it smoothly and without the audience seeing the secret compartment!

mix and match

Since you have two handkerchiefs in your APPEARING AND DISAPPEARING KIT, you can do a fun variation on this trick. Hide the first handkerchief in your pocket. Take the second handkerchief and stuff it into the secret compartment as the audience watches—pretend to be just putting it inside the box. Take the box apart, hiding the secret compartment as you did in step 6. The handkerchief is gone! Make the handkerchief "reappear" in your pocket—that is, pull the first handkerchief out of your pocket. Since the handkerchiefs are identical, your audience will think it's the same one you made disappear!

> **Trick Tip:** It's fun to take two different tricks and link them together. It helps your act flow smoothly, and it makes you look like a better magician. Here's how: Make one of your props "appear" in **The Black Hole**. Now jump into another trick, using the prop you just got!

assignment: To make a handkerchief disappear into your bare hand and then make it reappear!

my new finger

With this trick, you have a hiding place right in your own hand! It's called a Digitip, and it's a fake fingertip that's hollow. The handkerchief fits right inside, and no one can tell where it's gone!

from your appearing and disappearing kit: Blue silk handkerchief, Digitip

backstage

Pick up the Digitip and place it on your right thumb. That's it. Now you've got a case of "fake fingeritis"!

show time!

"Here's a blue silk handkerchief. It was made by Silky, a very talented silk-worm."

> **Trick Tip:** Feel free to move the tip from finger to finger until you find one that fits. Try your thumb or your index finger or your middle finger or your...you get the idea! Also, don't worry if the Digitip doesn't match your skin tone—if you do this trick right, no one should see the Digitip anyway!

STEP 1: Hold up the ends of the handkerchief between your fingers. Your Digitip thumb should be hidden behind the corner of the handkerchief.

"The handkerchief is blue, but do you know what color the silkworm is? It's impossible to see, 'cause he's invisible."

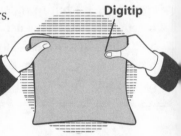

Digitip

MAGICIAN'S VIEW

STEP 2: Drop the handkerchief from your left hand so that only your right hand is holding it by the corner. Your left hand should look like it's holding the invisible silkworm! And you should be looking at your left hand. Your Digitip thumb should still be hidden behind the handkerchief.

"But I have him here, squirmin' around in my hand."

STEP 3: Turn your body so that your right side is facing the audience. Drape the handkerchief over your left wrist, keeping your Digitip thumb behind the handkerchief.

"Watch. The silkworm is going to do his magic inside my closed hand. Remember, my hand has four fingers and a thumb."

STEP 4: Keeping the handkerchief draped over your left wrist, slide your right thumb (still wearing the Digitip) from behind the handkerchief and into your right palm, so it's hidden behind your fingers. Point to the little finger of your left hand and count.

"One."

STEP 5: This counting procedure sets up the misdirection that lets you secretly put the Digitip in your left hand. Point to your ring finger.

"Two."

AUDIENCE'S VIEW

STEP 6: Point to your middle finger.

"Three."

STEP 7: Point to your index finger.

"Four fingers."

STEP 8: Turn your left hand so its thumb is pointing down.

"Wait...there's one more..."

STEP 9: Your right thumb and the Digitip should now be behind your left palm. Close your left fingers around the Digitip and move your right hand down, taking off the

Digitip. Point to your left thumb with your right index finger and say:

"...and a thumb."

STEP 10: Congratulations, that was "thumb-thing" else! You just secretly snuck the Digitip into your left hand! Now turn your body so you are facing your audience straight on again. Hold your left hand in front of you. It should be closed into a fist so that it hides the Digitip. Grab the handkerchief with your right hand.

"Now watch the invisible silkworm do his magic. He can turn the handkerchief into any color."

STEP 11: Stuff the handkerchief into the Digitip using different fingers of your right hand. First stuff a little bit of the handkerchief with your right index finger, then your right middle finger, then your fourth finger. This is all part of the misdirection that'll let you replace the Digitip on your thumb in step 13.

"What color would you like the handkerchief to become?"

STEP 12: The audience will name any color. Let's say green, just as an example. (Psst! It doesn't matter what color they call out; we're going to play a little joke on them!)

"Green? Let's see if the worm can do it!"

STEP 13: The handkerchief should be completely stuffed into the Digitip. Now, push your thumb into the Digitip, and withdraw it from your left fist. Your audience watched you use all your fingers to push the handkerchief inside your hand, so this looks totally natural.

"On the count of three. Ready? One, two..."

STEP 14: Let your right fingertips drop down, shielding the view of the Digitip from your audience. Keep your left fist closed so that it looks as though it still has the handkerchief in it.

"...three. Yes, there it is."

STEP 15: Say it with pride! You know you've got nothing in your left hand, but let the audience think you really do! (It's invisible! Get it? Great joke, huh?)

"A beautiful invisible green silk handkerchief!"

STEP 16: Turn and face your audience, and shake the "invisible" handkerchief. (Don't worry about your audience seeing the Digitip on your right thumb. They'll be looking at your moving left hand.)

"Okay, now the magic silkworm is going to change it back."

STEP 17: Make a fist again with your left hand, and insert your right thumb and the Digitip (with the blue handkerchief in it) into your hand. Slip the Digitip off your right thumb, leaving it inside your left fist.

"Let's see how he's done."

STEP 18: Now that the Digitip is in your left hand, pull the handkerchief from the Digitip with your right thumb and index finger.

"Amazing, isn't it? That's one tricky silkworm!"

STEP 19: Drape the handkerchief over your left hand as you open your left hand slowly. This hides the Digitip under the handkerchief. Take your bow. You're done!

HOMEWORK: Practice the counting technique and turning your left hand down as you steal the Digitip from your right thumb. The counting and the movements should be even and unhurried so no one suspects you are doing anything sneaky.

extra credit: Here's a fun bit of trickery. Take a dollar bill and fold it into a teeny, tiny rectangle. Press it into your closed fist, which is hiding the Digitip, and stuff the dollar bill into the Digitip! When you open your hand, the dollar's gone! This is a great way to boost your allowance!

super extra credit: This one's even better. Before you start, fold up a dollar bill in your right hand, and place it next to the Digitip, which is also in your hand. Close up your hand into a fist. Take one or two coins from someone in the audience and stuff them into your fist (but really put them inside the Digitip). Quickly pass your left hand over your right hand, and remove the Digitip (and the coins). When you open your right hand, it looks like the coins have turned into a dollar!

Now try it this way!

Here's a variation you can do with the Digitip and both hand-kerchiefs. Before the show, secretly place one of the duplicate handkerchiefs in the pocket of someone in the audience. After you hide the first handkerchief in your Digitip, have your audience member reach into his pocket and pull out the duplicate—everyone'll think it traveled across the room! Everyone who's gullible, that is!

THUMB THING

Originally called a Thumb Tip, the Digitip was first made of metal and was invented by Professor Herwin in England around 1885. The thumb tip he actually used is on display at the Museum of the Magic Circle in London.

The Digitip has been used by phony psychics to switch pieces of paper so they could secretly read their client's questions.

Today, magicians use the Digitip for all kinds of tricks, like making a dollar bill appear inside a lemon after the money has been placed into an envelope!

---

assignment: Make balls appear, disappear, and multiply!

dodgeball

Sponge balls are like overcooked broccoli—they're all soft and squishy. And while you can't do any magic tricks with soggy green vegetables, you can work wonders with sponge balls! Their squishiness lets you hide them in your hands so it looks like they've disappeared. And when you unsquish 'em, they seem to appear out of nowhere!

magic must-haves: Magic trunk

from your appearing and disappearing kit: Four sponge balls

extras: A volunteer who doesn't know the trick

backstage

Take two of the sponge balls (we'll call them #3 and #4) and place them in your right-hand pants pocket. Take another sponge ball (let's call it sponge

> **Trick Tip:** Because of their unique squishiness, sponge balls make great objects to hide inside the Black Box.

ball #1) and hold it in your right hand between your thumb and index finger, just like you were showing it to the audience. Take the last sponge ball (let's call it sponge ball #2), and hide it under the curled-up middle, ring, and pinky fingers of your right hand. You are ready for some sponge magic!

show time!

STEP 1: Place sponge ball #1 on the magic trunk.

"Look, I have a ball made of sponge. Come on up here, and test it for yourself."

STEP 2: Once your volunteer has squashed it and proved that it's really a sponge ball, you get to do the tricky part. Place your right hand, palm down, on top of sponge ball #1. As you open your hand, you'll secretly release sponge ball #2, which you should press against sponge ball #1.

"That was pretty good, but I guess you didn't realize that this sponge ball is really a magic ball..."

STEP 3: Slowly roll the two sponge balls over the magic trunk. Ease up on the pressure, and lift your hand. To the audience, it will look like one sponge ball has magically divided into two! (Once you've trained them properly, an audience is oh-so-easily fooled!)

"...that can divide in two, among other things."

STEP 4: Pick up one of the sponge balls on the trunk with your right hand. Now you're about to perform what magicians call a *retention vanish*. You pretend that you're moving a ball from your right hand to your left, but you'll really keep the ball in your right hand. Don't worry—we'll explain as we go along.

"I'll put..."

AUDIENCE'S VIEW

STEP 5: Get ready—here comes the ol' retention vanish! Hold the sponge ball at the tips of your right fingers. Hold your left-hand palm open, like it's ready to "receive" the ball.

MAGICIAN'S VIEW

"...one of the balls..."

STEP 6: Move your hands closer together. Overlap your hands, and start curling your left fingers around your right fingertips and the sponge ball.

"...in my left hand."

STEP 7: Close your left hand, squeezing together your right thumb and fingers around the sponge ball. Now pull your right hand away from your left, taking the ball with you. By using your right thumb to squish the sponge ball against your right fingers, your right hand should be hiding the ball from the audience, who will think that the sponge ball is now in your left hand.

MAGICIAN'S VIEW

"I need a volunteer from the audience."

STEP 8: As you look around for a volunteer, use your right hand to immediately pick up the second sponge ball from the magic trunk and squish it against the first sponge ball. Because you've squished the two balls together, it should look like you are holding just one ball!

"All right. You. Come on up."

STEP 9: Call up your volunteer, and have him hold his right hand palm up.

"I'll put one sponge ball in your hand."

STEP 10: Place both sponge balls in his hand and tell him to squeeze his hand into a fist. Keep your left hand closed tight—remember, everyone thinks there's a ball in there! Make sure his hand is closing before you completely let go of the balls. (Hey, and if your volunteer is having some difficulty comprehending the idea of closing his hand, press his hand together for him—you're not going to let a bad volunteer spoil your magic!) Once his hand is closed, turn his hand so that the back of his hand is facing up. This will make it a lot less likely that he will look in his hand or open his hand before you want him to.

"Now hold on to this ball tightly, and don't let go."

STEP 11: Blow on your left hand.

"Let's see what happened."

STEP 12: Open your left hand, and show the audience that it's empty!

"Blow on your right hand, [volunteer's name]. Where's *your sponge ball?*"

STEP 13: Your volunteer opens his right hand. Surprise! He's got two sponge balls in it!

"How about that! You have both of them! Those magic balls sure are sneaky."

STEP 14: You can stop the trick here, but why, when you're doing so well? So let's go on. While the audience reacts to the surprise appearance of sponge ball #1 and sponge ball #2, reach into your right pocket and secretly pull out sponge ball #3. Hide it like you hid sponge ball #2 at the beginning of the trick—curling your middle, ring, and pinky fingers around it.

"Cool, huh? Now put both balls back down on the magic trunk, here."

STEP 15: Keeping sponge ball #3 hidden in your right hand, pick up sponge ball #1 from the magic trunk with your right hand.

"This is a pretty simple sponge ball math problem."

STEP 16: Place sponge ball #1 and sponge ball #3 into your left hand—really place them there this time! But the audience shoul only see you placing sponge ball #1!

"If I take one sponge ball..."

STEP 17: Pick up sponge ball #2 from the magic trunk, using your right hand.

"...and add it to another sponge ball..."

STEP 18: All right, let's review: You now have one visible sponge ball in your left hand (sponge ball #1); one ball visible in your right hand (sponge ball #2); oh, and one ball hidden in your left hand (sponge ball #3).

"...and I throw in an invisible sponge ball..."

MAGICIAN'S VIEW

STEP 19: Reach down to the magic trunk with your right hand, and pretend to pick up an invisible sponge ball. Toss it—invisibly—into your closed left hand.

"...how many sponge balls does that give me?"

STEP 20: If the audience guesses correctly, congratulate them, open your hands, and roll out the three balls onto the magic trunk. If they're wrong, say:

"You guys aren't very good at sponge ball math."

STEP 21: Roll out the three sponge balls onto the magic trunk. While everyone reacts to the appearance of the third sponge ball, reach into your right-hand pocket, and secretly take out sponge ball #4.

"Let's try some more sponge ball math and see how we do."

STEP 22: Using your right hand, pick up sponge balls #1, #2, and #3 from the magic trunk. Now you have four sponge balls in your right hand, but the audience thinks you have only three. You can keep one between your thumb and index finger, but hide the others under your curled middle, ring, and pinky fingers.

"But I want a different volunteer this time."

STEP 23: After your volunteer steps forward—

"Please hold your hand open like this."

STEP 24: —gesture with your left hand open, palm up. After your volunteer does the same, place all four sponge balls into her hand. Make sure her hand is closing before you let go of the four balls. Turn her hand palm down, so she won't be tempted to look in her hand and find out she's holding four balls—not the three she thinks she has!

"Now squeeze these three sponge balls together very tightly."

STEP 25: Instruct her to blow on her closed left hand.

"Now, open up, and let's see what you've got."

STEP 26: When she opens her hands, four sponge balls will roll out! Sponge ball math wins again!

homework

You guessed it—being able to hide the sponge balls is essential to this trick. Practice holding sponge balls curled up under your middle, ring, and pinky fingers so that when you look in the mirror, it looks like you're not holding anything.

extra credit: When you're really confident with the retention vanish—making the sponge ball look like it's moved to one hand when it really hasn't moved at all—you can make the "vanished" ball appear in your pocket, your friend's pocket, in a cup—anywhere you can imagine. Just make sure you make it "reappear" quickly before your audience has time to suspect that it may be hidden in your right hand.

super extra credit: You can also make a sponge ball appear or disappear inside the Digitip. It stuffs in there just like the handkerchief trick, but the cool thing is that when you pull the sponge ball out, you can use a pair of tweezers—it looks funny, and it helps grab the sponge ball without making you look like a doofus.

ABSORBENT MAGIC

Balls have been a magician's best friend for hundreds of years. But after sponge rubber was invented back in 1886, Jesse Lybarger added sponge ball tricks to his routine in 1926.

That same year another magician, Joe Berg, used sponge balls in the classic Cups and Balls trick. (You remember learning Cups and Balls, right? In *The Book of Illusions*?) Ten years later, Audley Walsh made sponge balls really popular with his book *Spongeball Manipulation*.

In the first half of the twentieth century, magicians made their own sponge balls by individually carving them out of sponge rubber blocks. That was a heck of a lot of work, so in the 1960s, Al Stevenson figured out a way to manufacture nearly perfect spheres from polyurethane foam. Isn't progress great?

WHERE'S my SUGAR? # 7

assignment: Make a sugar cube vanish from under a handkerchief!

the sugar thief

Who's your buddy? Who's your pal? Who's your bestest best friend ever? If you don't know, get one now because you'll need one. He's the person who actually steals the sugar cube right from under everyone's nose!

magic must-haves: Magic trunk

from your appearing and disappearing kit: Handkerchief

Homemade magic: A glass of water and a sugar cube

extras: Don't forget your best friend (magicians call him a *confederate*)

> **Trick Tip:** If you don't have a sugar cube, you can also use a grape, or a coin, or a die. Anything that's about that same size works great!

backstage

You're going to use this time to prep your confederate and let him in on the trick's secret. It's all going to depend on him to get it right. And make sure that once you reveal the secret to him, he keeps it to himself—forever! After all, that's the Magician's Code, right? Oh, and one other thing: Be sure you don't eat the sugar cube before your performance!

Now you're ready to start. Place the sugar cube, the handkerchief, and the glass of water on the magic trunk.

show time!

"Did you ever watch a sugar cube dissolve into nothing when you put it underwater? Cool, huh? But I can do it one better. I can make a sugar cube dissolve so fast you won't be able to see it happening."

STEP 1: Make sure you know which is your right hand and which is your left hand. Once you've got that figured out, hold

out the sugar cube in your right hand. Pick up the handkerchief with your left hand, and place it over the sugar cube like a blanket. Make sure the sugar cube is covered up!

"I've got a sugar cube in my right hand. First, I'll cover up the sugar cube with this ordinary handkerchief."

STEP 2: Ask different people in the audience to put their hand underneath the handkerchief and feel the cube.

"Come on up, one at a time, and feel the cube underneath the handkerchief. See? It's still there."

STEP 3: After a few people have felt the cube and confirmed its existence, call up your confederate (you know, the friend who's in on the secret), and ask him to feel the cube. He's the last person who's going to feel it!

"Okay, now I want [your confederate's name] to come up here and touch the sugar cube."

STEP 4: While your confederate does this, turn to the other members of your audience and engage in a classic misdirection (check out the details in step 5). The idea is that you're going to get their attention while your confederate palms the cube! The palming is easy: He lays his hand flat on the sugar cube and grips it tight between his thumb and the side of his hand. Then he slides his hand out from under the

> **Trick Tip:** Make sure your confederate is wearing pants with pockets for this trick! It also helps if the pants are a little baggy so the audience can't see the outline of the cube. Duh!

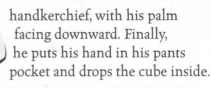

handkerchief, with his palm facing downward. Finally, he puts his hand in his pants pocket and drops the cube inside.

"Now, let me see a show of hands. Who wants to see the sugar cube dissolve today?"

STEP 5: Okay, here's the skinny on the misdirection. As the audience's hands go up and they answer your question, that's when your confederate is removing the cube and casually dropping it in his pocket. But your confederate should never stop watching you! If he's watching his hands, he's giving away the secret!

"All right. It looks like everyone wants to see it dissolve fast."

STEP 6: Now that you have their answer, pick up the glass of water from the magic trunk with your left hand (your right hand should still be covered by the handkerchief). Wave the glass over the top of the handkerchief.

"Remember when I said that a sugar cube dissolves underwater? I'll hold this glass of water so that the sugar is 'under it.' Get it? Under the water!"

STEP 7: Return the glass to the magic trunk. Now grab one of the corners of the handkerchief with your left hand, and yank the handkerchief off your right hand. Oh, no! The sugar cube is gone. Hold your hand flat and turn it over a couple of times so everyone can see it. (If you forgot to wash your hands before doing the trick, make sure your mom isn't in the audience.)

Trick Tip: A lot of magic tricks can have more than one ending. One great tricky ending is to have a second sugar cube in your pocket. When people ask what happened to the sugar cube, reach into your pocket and pull out your duplicate! That's the great thing about sugar cubes: They all look alike.

If you want to be really tricky and you're feeling like you've got this trick nailed, try slipping the duplicate cube into the pocket of one of your friends. (He doesn't have to be in on the trick—it works better if you can just drop it into his pocket sneakily.) As you do the trick, tell the audience that you're going to make the sugar cube reappear in someone's pocket. Then look around the room at the end of the trick as if you're trying to figure out who has it. When you tell the chosen one to look in his pocket, won't he be surprised!

Homework: You and your confederate need to practice working together a few times first, to make sure your friend can palm the sugar cube easily without his hand looking "funny." Once you have a good confederate on your side, you can train him like a dog to help you in other tricks. (But you probably won't have to take him out for walks.)

THE CONFIDENT CONFEDERATE

Using secret assistants who pretend to be members of the audience is one of the most closely guarded secrets in magic. Good thing you're enrolled in Magic U., so we can tell you all about it. Back in the 1930s, Harry Blackstone used confederates for his Pickpocket Trick. During the show, he'd call them up onstage and remove watches, wallets, belts, and neckties from them, with each one claiming he "didn't feel a thing!"

ace up! #8

assignment: Make hidden aces rise to the top of a deck of cards!

those traveling aces

This is one of those great magic tricks that does all the work for you because of classic misdirection! All you're really doing is just moving the four top cards (the aces) to the tops of different piles. The constant cutting of the deck is just busy work—it makes the audience think you're doing more than you really are!

magic must-haves:
Magic trunk

homemade magic: A
deck of normal playing cards

extras: You'll need a volunteer who doesn't know the trick. So she's no confederate!

> **Trick Tip:** You can use the marked deck from your Mentalism Kit, but you can also use a friend's deck of cards. That makes the trick even more amazing ('cause your friend's sure *his* deck's not gimmicked). Just make sure any deck you use has all four aces!

backstage
Pull out the four aces from the deck, and put them facedown on top of the deck, which is also facedown.

show time!
"Aces are the world travelers in a deck of cards. But they don't go to places like France or Spain or Hawaii. They move around in the deck, trying to reach the top. Let me show you."

STEP 1: Place the deck on the magic trunk, facedown to your left. This is just one more reason why it's so important to know your left from your right.

"What's really amazing about this is that the aces travel all by themselves. I don't have to do anything except make a few travel arrangements."

STEP 2: Call up a volunteer from the audience. Don't tell her anything about the trick; let her be just as surprised as the audience. It helps if she knows left from right, too. Have her stand or sit opposite you.

"I want you to cut the deck. But don't do it evenly. Make sure that the top section of the deck is bigger than the bottom section. Place the larger part facedown to the left of the smaller part."

STEP 3: After your volunteer cuts the deck, she has another job to perform. Point to the top card of the larger pile on your right (the audience's left).

"Now take the top card from the larger pile and put it on the top of the smaller pile."

STEP 4: After your volunteer moves the top card from the pile on your right to the pile on your left, point back to the pile on your right.

"Now, cut this pile. Again, the top part should be larger than the bottom part. Leave the bottom, smaller part where it is on the trunk, and put the top, larger part to the left of that."

STEP 5: You now have three piles of cards, and we're nowhere near done yet! You might say this is going to be a multicard pileup!

"Now, I want you to take the top card from the pile that's all the way to your left and place it on what is now the middle pile."

STEP 6: Now, point to the pile that's all the way to your right (the audience's left).

"So far, so good. Now, cut this pile unevenly; again, the top part should be larger than the bottom part. Leave the bottom part of the pile where it is on the trunk and put the top part to the left of that."

STEP 7: When your volunteer finishes, you should have four piles of cards facedown on the magic trunk.

"Take the top card off the new pile that's all the way to your left, and place it on top of the pile that's just to the right of it— that's the pile that's third from your right."

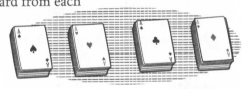

STEP 8: If you've done this correctly and your volunteer did everything just the way you told her, then you're ready for the final bit. You should have four stacks of cards facedown on the magic trunk. (If not, pretend your mother's calling you home for dinner, pick up the cards, and go!)

"Okay, let's see where those aces traveled to this time."

STEP 9: Flip over the top card from each pile. Each one is an ace.

"And remember, I didn't even touch the cards! You did everything!"

HOMEWORK: This is a fun assignment. Practice cutting the cards into piles and moving the top card to the previous stack. The key to the trick is to keep the cards moving so the audience really believes the aces are traveling from different places in the deck!

kNot it!

assignment: Knot a piece of rope in midair!

tying the knot

This is one of those great tricks that works itself. All you have to do is place the rope the right way in your hand and rotate your hand correctly. The knot takes care of itself. (Knots are very independent.)

homemade magic: Yee-hah! Git yerself a good 3-foot piece of rope, pardner.

backstage

Rope tricks are like gymnasts—they only work if they're really flexible. We don't know how gymnasts do it, but here's an easy way to loosen up a piece of rope: Just keep washing it in the washing machine and drying it in the dryer. Do it until the rope is really, really soft.

show time!

"My parents wouldn't let me have a dog. But they were nice enough to get me a pet rope for my birthday."

STEP 1: Dangle the rope in front of your audience.

"At first I was kind of annoyed, but then I figured I could train my pet rope just like it was a dog."

STEP 2: Put the rope on the table in front of you (or on the floor if pets aren't allowed on the furniture).

"Okay, Roper. Stay! Good boy!"

STEP 3: Look at your audience as though they should be impressed with your pet rope's obedience. They might groan or laugh.

"Now watch this. Roper! Roll over! Do you hear me? Roll over!"

STEP 4: When the rope doesn't move, grab one end and turn it over. The rest of the rope will follow. (If the rope turns over on its own, then you really do have a magic rope and you should pack your bags and join the circus!)

"Hey, that's pretty good, right?"

STEP 5: By now your audience should be looking at you like you've lost your mind. That's a good thing, 'cause it prepares them for this next part.

"Okay, if you aren't impressed by any of that, I guess Roper and I will have to do our special trick. We only learned it yesterday, but I think he can do it. It just requires a special command."

STEP 6: Drape the rope over the palm of your right hand. End A should hang between your ring finger (that's the finger next to your pinky, in case you fell asleep during Finger Class) and your pinky. End B should hang between your thumb and index finger (that's the one you pick your nose with, even though you shouldn't). Now, end A may be any length, but end B shouldn't be more than one foot below your hand.

"Okay, I think that Roper's ready. On the count of three, Roper! One... two... three... knot!"

STEP 7: This is the part of the trick that has to be done quickly and smoothly. Turn your right hand palm down, and grab length B between your first and second fingers. The trick here is that you may have to swing the ends of the rope in order to catch length B between your fingertips; or you can rotate your hand sharply downward to grab length B— whichever's easier for you! Now all you have to do is let the loop that has been formed around your right hand fall off your hand. The end of length B will be drawn through this loop, forming a knot in the rope. You can also snap the rope off your hand by pulling one end with your left hand rather than letting the rope fall.

"Good boy, Roper! Good boy!"

HOMEWORK: You might have guessed that the looping and grabbing of the rope is the tricky part. Stand in front of a mirror and practice your hand-rope action until it's as smooth as taking the lid off a juice bottle. It has to be fast enough that the audience doesn't catch on.

Trick Tip 1: You can add some more flair to this trick with this little bit of business. Once you have length B firmly between your first and second fingers on your right hand, throw the rope straight up into the air. But don't let go of length B until it's passed through the loop. This creates the illusion that the knot was tied in midair!

Trick Tip 2: You can also hold onto the end of length B and twirl the rope in a circle 'round and 'round until the rope is dizzy. The knot will tighten, and because the rope's moving, your audience won't see it until the rope stops.

THE DUMBO DROP

It's not easy working with wild animals, but magicians have been making elephants disappear for decades. It took Siegfried and Roy, the magical duo who have been performing in Las Vegas shows for the past twenty-five years, to make an elephant vanish and reappear in the same routine.

The audience sees a large round platform in the center of the stage with an elephant on it. A row of dancers stands behind the platform. Roy climbs atop the beast and grabs a rope that hangs from the ceiling. A very large curtain is raised around the pachyderm (that's a fancy word for elephant—we hate to repeat ourselves!), but we can still see Roy peeking out from over the curtain. Suddenly, the curtain drops. The elephant is gone and Roy is hanging on for dear life! The rope is quickly lowered to the stage, and Roy gestures for the curtain to be raised up. The curtain is raised, and then it falls quickly to the floor again, revealing the elephant, which has reappeared!

matcHBOX moNey! #10

assiGNMeNt: Make a nickel appear inside an empty matchbox!

BURIeD tReasURe

The key to this trick is easy—the nickel is hidden inside the matchbox, but the audience doesn't know it. They think the box is empty because they can't see the coin.

HoMeMaDe MaGic: One

matchbox with the matches removed (your parents can do this for you), one nickel (hit your parents up for that, too!)

sleeve

drawer

BaCKstaGe

Take the nickel, and wedge it inside the back of the matchbox, between the top of the drawer and the sleeve. (The sleeve is the thing that the little drawer slides in and out of.) The nickel shouldn't actually be in the drawer, just on top of it. It will stick out a little bit from the end of the match-box. It's easier to wedge the nickel inside the matchbox when the drawer is upside down. Make sure the drawer is right side up when you start the trick, though.

sHoW time!

"You should never play with matches, you know. That's why the matchbox that I have here is empty."

STEP 1: Show the audience that the matchbox is empty (even though it really isn't) by slowly pulling the drawer out of the sleeve. You can do it fast if you want, but then the nickel will fall out and all you can do is yell *"Free nickel!"* and go home. And be sure not to pull the drawer all the way out of the sleeve, 'cause then the nickel's sure to fall out.

"But I can make something appear in it with your help."

STEP 2: Shake the box really gently. If the coin is wedged tightly between the drawer and the sleeve, it won't move, and the lack of a rattling noise will "prove" to the audience that there's nothing in the matchbox.

"Repeat after me: 'MONEY! MONEY! MONEY!'"

STEP 3: After the audience has repeated your magic words, snap the drawer quickly back into the sleeve, closing the matchbox. If you've wedged the nickel in correctly, this quick-shutting method will dislodge the nickel and plop it into the drawer.

"I think that did the job."

STEP 4: Shake the box. It should rattle like there's a nickel inside!

"Hear it? I think we have a winner!"

STEP 5: Now the fun part—you can either open the box yourself or hand it to someone in the audience to open it for you. Either way, once it's open, there'll be a nickel inside!

HOMEWORK: If you've been paying attention you know that the wedging of the nickel is all-important. Once you've got the nickel where you want it, practice pulling out the drawer so that the coin doesn't fall out. Then snap the drawer shut so you can dislodge the nickel. With practice, you'll find a speed that works for you!

> **Trick Tip:** Big-time professional magicians often combine two tricks to make an even bigger one. Find a Magic University trick where you make a coin disappear under a glass or handkerchief (say, **Where's My Sugar?**—but use a coin instead of a sugar cube), then make it reappear inside the matchbox. All you need is two coins, one of them already hidden inside the matchbox.

SHIFTING GEARS

As soon as the car was invented in the 1900s, it found its way into magic tricks as well. Many of the great touring magicians of the vaudeville era included a trick that involved making a car disappear as part of their show.

More recently, Joseph Gabriel made a yellow Checker taxicab appear onstage. Lance Burton makes a Chevrolet Corvette appear nightly in his Las Vegas show at the Monte Carlo Hotel.

RHyme time! #11

assignment: Make postage stamps disappear while you sing (no, really)!

Sing a happy song

It's hard to believe that this trick actually fools people, but it does. They never realize that you're using different fingers because they're so busy looking for the mysterious "birdies" you keep talking about. The secret? Speed. This whole trick shouldn't take more than fifteen seconds.

homemade magic: Two self-stick postage stamps (and two middle fingers) and a table

> **Trick Tip:** You can get all kinds of postage stamps from your local post office. Try to get the smallest you can with either pictures of birds (like the American eagle) or airplanes. If you can't get stamps, tear two small pieces of paper from the flap of an envelope. Lick the gummed side and stick them to your fingernails as described in **BACKSTAGE**.

Backstage

First, you have to memorize this goofy children's nursery rhyme. Don't worry—it parallels the trick. Honest!

"Two little birdies, sitting on a wall. One is named Peter. The other's named Paul. Fly away, Peter! Fly away, Paul! Come back, Peter! Come back, Paul! Two little birdies, sitting on a wall."

Once you've memorized the rhyme, lick two postage stamps or pieces of envelope flap, and stick them to the fingernail of your middle finger on both hands. Now, address yourself to France and see how far you get. Just kidding. If you're sure you've memorized the rhyme, you're ready to go!

Show time!

"Not only am I going to do a magic trick, I'm going to tell you a story and sing a little song. Don't worry, it won't be too off-key. Here we go: Two little birdies..."

MAGICIAN'S VIEW

STEP 1: Put both of your middle fingers on the table edge, and hold your other fingertips below the table edge. The audience sitting across from you should only be able to see your middle fingers with the stamps on your fingernails. All your other fingers are hidden!

"...sitting on a wall."

STEP 2: Tap your left middle finger on the table a few times and say:

"One is named Peter. "

STEP 3: Tap your right middle finger on the table a few times and say:

AUDIENCE'S VIEW

"The other's named Paul."

STEP 4: Didn't know your fingers had names, did you? Now lift your left hand into the air quickly, and fold your middle, ring, and little fingers against your palm, while extending your index finger. Immediately bring your left hand back to the table, but put your index finger (the one without a stamp) on the table's edge. Your other fingers, including the middle one with the stamp, should be hiding under the table as before. The audience will think the finger you've just put on the table is the same one that you raised from the table! Here's the catch: You have to do all of this while you say just three words:

"Fly away, Peter!"

STEP 5: Repeat step 4, only now use your right hand instead of your left. Say these three words:

"Fly away, Paul!"

41

STEP 6: You should now have two index fingers (both without stamps) resting on the edge of the table. All your other fingers should be hidden from the audience. Now, reverse the move you made in step 4. Throw your left hand up in the air, curl your index finger into your palm, and stick out your middle finger (the one with the stamp). Then bring it down on the table so that your middle finger rests on the edge of the table and your other fingers are hidden. Do this as you say:

"Come back, Peter!"

STEP 7: Repeat step 6, using your right hand. Throw your right hand up in the air, curl your index finger into your palm, and stick out your middle finger (the one with the stamp). Then bring your middle finger down on the table so that it rests on the edge and your other fingers are hidden. Do this as you say:

"Come back, Paul!"

STEP 8: You're back where you started. Both middle fingers and stamps are showing, and your other fingers are hidden. Now wrap it up by repeating:

"Two little birdies, sitting on a wall."

HOMEWORK: Practice the rhyme and your fast finger-work!

PRIME RHYME TIME

Magicians have been using rhyming patter for centuries. It adds so much to a performance when you can recite a poem well and do a trick that relates to it. The most famous performer to use rhyming patter was the American magician Dell O'Dell, who performed from 1930 to 1950. She was the leading female magician of her time and was probably a lot of fun at parties!

Pencil? What Pencil? #12

assignment: Make a pencil disappear from under a handkerchief!

write this down

This is so cool! What the audience thinks they're seeing under the handkerchief is a pencil, but it's really your index finger. While you're working your patter, you've already slipped the pencil down the sleeve of your shirt.

magic must-haves: Magic trunk

homemade magic: A cloth handkerchief,
bandanna or napkin (your silk handkerchief is too small), an unsharpened pencil, and a jacket or shirt with long sleeves

backstage

This one's a breeze. Just relax. Take a deep breath if you want. Then calmly set the handkerchief and the pencil down on the magic trunk. Oh, and make sure you're wearing your long sleeves, too.

show time!

"I don't know how it is at your house, but at mine, we can never find a pencil to write with."

STEP 1: If you can do two things at once, show the audience the pencil in your right hand while you hold the handkerchief in your left.

"Whenever we need one, there's never one around. I think I know why."

STEP 2: Hold the pencil between your right thumb and right middle finger. Your fingertips should be near the top of the pencil, with the eraser pointing to the ceiling. Your left hand now drapes the handkerchief over your right, covering the pencil.

43

"During the night, when the house is totally dark..."

STEP 3: Raise your forearm (the part of your arm between your elbow and your hand) so that it's vertical. Your whole arm should be in an L shape. As you do this, extend your right index finger so that it holds up the handkerchief and appears to be the pencil. Tricky, huh? The (unsharpened) pencil tip should be directly over the open sleeve of your jacket or long-sleeved shirt.

"...the pencils come out in their costumes and dance like crazy."

STEP 4: Move your right index finger so that the audience thinks the pencil is dancing.

"It's a wild and wonderful dance, but it has one interesting side effect."

STEP 5: When the pencil tip is directly over your open sleeve (you should be able to feel it with your wrist), let the pencil go. It will fall into your sleeve. Don't worry—the hanky will hide this action. You may have to raise your hand just a little— not too much—to make the pencil slide all the way down to your elbow. Whoosh! Pencil's gone! Aren't you glad it's unsharpened? You saved your arm from being poked full of lead!

"The pencils get so dizzy..."

STEP 6: With your left hand, whip off the handkerchief. At the same time, hold out your open right hand to the audience.

"...they totally disappear!"

HOMEWORK: Practice dropping the pencil down your sleeve. You've got to do it without looking and without dropping it on the floor!

Trick Tip: This is a good trick with which to end your act. You've still got a pencil hidden in your sleeve and you don't want it to fall out while you're doing another trick.

THE LONG AND THE SHORT OF SLEEVES

Sleeving has nothing to do with making clothes. It's what the big-time magicians call the art of sneaking something into their sleeve to make it seem like it disappeared (like you just did with the pencil). Magicians don't use it as often as people think they do, but it's still very effective with small objects like coins, pencils, and magic wands. The two recognized masters at sleeving were Jack Chanin and Emil Jarrow. Who would have thought that someone would actually have published an entire *Encyclopedia of Sleeving*? Chanin did, in 1947. Well before then (by the 1920's) Jarrow could sleeve powdery substances like salt or sand without spilling a grain! Don't try that in your own kitchen!

PiPs aHoy! #13

assignment: Make the pips on a bunch of playing cards disappear!

which way did they go?

The trick here is that you aren't really making anything disappear in the traditional sense. Through careful manipulation of the cards, you're hiding the markings to make it seem like the cards are blank!

magic must-haves: Magic trunk

Homemade magic: A deck of normal playing cards

it's a pip!

Just what is a *pip*? Well, if you're a professional card player, you already know what pips are, so you can skip this part.

> **Trick Tip:** If you can use a friend's deck of cards, this trick will seem even more amazing. He might believe you rigged your own cards, but not his!

For the rest of you, a pip is the little icon on the card—the spade, the heart, the club, or the diamond.

backstage

This trick requires learning an easy process called the *reverse fan*, which has nothing to do with air-conditioning. It's a card move. The reverse fan is created by spreading the deck of cards from left to right, instead of right to left.

show time!

"I always get bored in the doctor's office."

STEP 1: Pick up the deck from the magic trunk. Take out between fifteen and thirty cards. Whatever you do, make sure that you've taken out at least one of the following aces in your stack: the ace of clubs, ace of hearts, or ace of diamonds (not the ace of spades). Put the remaining cards to the side. Hold your stack in both hands, and fan the cards normally. Normally doesn't mean the reverse fan move. That's coming up soon. Don't let your audience see the faces of the cards.

"So I like to take some cards with me."

STEP 2: Turn the cards over in your hand, and spread them so you can see the faces. (If those faces are smiling, you picked up the wrong deck.) When you see one of the three aces (not the ace of spades), cut the deck at that spot so the ace is on the top of the deck where it is face up. The audience can see you cut the deck, but keep hiding the faces of the cards.

"One time, the doctor put the stethoscope to my chest and asked me to breathe."

STEP 3: Now it's time for the reverse fan.

"Then he asked me to take a deep breath."

STEP 4: Spread the cards on the back of the deck toward your right side. Make sure your audience can't see the faces of the cards as you spread them.

MAGICIAN'S VIEW *"I took such a deep breath..."*

STEP 5: Finish spreading the cards in a reverse fan. Be sure that you can't see any pips on the right sides of the cards.

"...that I sucked all the printing off the cards..."

STEP 6: Take a deep breath. As you do this, move your right hand so the thumb is covering the *index* on the lower right corner of the card. (The index is the number and pip at the corner of the card that tells you what card it is). The fingers of your right hand should be holding the packet of cards. Now adjust your left hand so the crotch of your thumb (the part where the bottom of your thumb meets the bottom of your index finger) covers the top left index of the ace and the tip of your thumb covers the larger diamond, heart, or club in the center of the ace. Want to know why you don't use the ace of spades? Your thumb is too small to cover the giant spade at the center of the ace of spades—that's why you don't use it.

"...until they looked like this."

STEP 7: Lower your hands so the cards are parallel to the ground and your friends can look down on the cards. They'll think they are blank! Wait a moment for the "blank" cards to make an impact on your audience.

"Freaky, huh? I thought I'd better fix them."

STEP 8: Raise the cards so the faces are toward you and the backs face the audience. Cut the deck so that you have two piles of cards, one of which doesn't have an ace on the face. Put the pile with the ace showing behind the other one.

"So I let out a big breath..."

STEP 9: Let out a big exhale in the direction of the cards. Lower the cards to show the audience that the pips are back in place.

"...and everything was back to normal."

STEP 10: Hand the cards to your audience to examine carefully. Since there are no blank cards, no one can figure this one out!

THE JOKE'S ON THEM!

Here's a variation that makes a great, quick practical joke. When you're at a friend's house and you spot a deck of cards, casually pick it up and flip through it. Put an ace on the face of the deck, and begin to reverse fan the deck as you say, *"This is the strangest deck I've ever seen. Do you play cards with these?"* Your friend will say something like, *"Yes, of course."* He's now fallen into your trap. Show him the blank cards and say, *"I don't know how! They all look alike to me!"* He'll probably burst into tears, and his mother will send you home, but that's life!

ANOTHER JOKE'S ON THEM!

If you ever have the chance to open a new deck of cards, you can put them into the proper reverse fan position and say, *"Oh, my, there must have been a mistake at the factory. No one can play with these cards. Look! They forgot to print them!"* Then say, *"I know; I'll work my magic."* Close up the fan, and hold the cards facedown as you wave one hand over the pack. Spread the cards normally to show that the pips have returned. *"Great. Now we can play with them."*

HOMEWORK: The fifteen-to-thirty card rule exists because that's the number of cards that can fit comfortably in your hand as you work the fan. If you keep practicing the fan and get more comfortable with it, start adding more cards. Just don't add so many that you start dropping them on the floor—that's a completely different trick!

ICE MAGIC

Max Malini was probably the greatest close-up magician of the twentieth century. Born Max Katz-Breit on the Polish-Austrian border in 1873, he studied magic in the United States as a teenager. He was very short and had tiny hands and spoke with a thick eastern European accent. But Malini used his odd physical appearance to develop a character that created real magic for his audiences.

continued…

By dressing impeccably and learning to perform for people in restaurants and bars, he became an expert in misdirection. He performed for three U.S. presidents and the heads of many European nations. He performed with everyday objects such as paper money, lemons, cups, corks, buttons, and coins. Once he approached a U.S. senator in Washington, D.C., tore a button off his coat and magically replaced it in an instant. He was immediately hired to entertain at fancy government parties.

But the most amazing trick Malini ever performed was for a group of magicians. At a fancy dinner given by a friend of magician and close-up magic expert Dai Vernon, Malini never once left the table. He apparently asked for the fancy French hat of one of the women present and said, in his heavily accented English, "Vatch, I'll show you a leetle trick." He spun a half-dollar on the table and covered it with the hat. He asked the woman to call out heads or tails. She guessed, and when Malini lifted the hat, the coin had disappeared, and in its place was a great block of ice.

What was particularly amazing about this feat of magic is that it was a warm summer day, and it was performed before indoor air-conditioning was invented. The appearance of the ice was amazing not only because no one saw him sneak it under the hat, but also because there was no place it could have been hidden through the dinner hour without melting!

tHE fRENCH dROP ENCORE #14

assignment: Make a quarter disappear from your hands!

drop it!

Sometimes it's called the *French Drop* and sometimes it's called *Le Tournequet.* Either way, you already learned it in *The Book of Illusions.* So you know there's only one secret to this trick and that's practice. This is a classic magician's sleight-of-hand move where the audience thinks the quarter is somewhere that it isn't. And you can only achieve that effect with a lot of hard work and some sweat. (And if you've forgotten this sleight, don't worry. We'll review it for you again.)

magic must-haves: Magic trunk

Homemade magic: Any small object, like a coin or a
small ball (one that's about the size of a rolled-up dollar bill—just don't use a rolled-up dollar bill!)

sHOW time—NOt!

This isn't really SHOW TIME! This is all practice and rehearsal-type stuff, so you can learn bigger and better tricks.

STEP 1: Hold the coin in full view in your left hand so everyone in your imaginary audience can see it. Use your middle finger and your thumb to hold it. Your left hand should be toward the left side of your body.

STEP 2: Turn the quarter so the audience can see both sides of it. (If you *had* an audience, and weren't just rehearsing)

STEP 3: Move both hands toward the center of your body, keeping the quarter in full view, your left hand palm up.

STEP 4: Now move your right hand in front of the fingertips of your left hand. When your right hand is positioned so that it hides your left, gently release your left thumb from the quarter. The quarter will drop back into your left hand.

STEP 5: Immediately close your right hand as though it's taking the quarter from your left hand.

STEP 6: Here's the trick: The quarter stays in your left hand. Lower your left hand as you hold the coin at the base of your left fingertips. Be careful not to close your left hand. Practice doing this so the quarter doesn't fall onto the floor. Continue to watch your right hand. Remember, your audience will look wherever you look!

STEP 7: Raise your right hand, or ask someone to wave his hand over yours. Open your right hand slowly. The quarter is gone! Congratulations, you've just done the basic French drop! And you didn't even have to learn the language to do it.

the new and improved french drop

Even though this move is a classic, there is a big problem with it. In order to do it, you have to hold your hands in a position that's not really natural. People may look at you and know that you're doing something "weird," because your hands are in an awkward position.

But once you learn the basic French drop, you're ready to change it and make it better.

the bell rings!

STEP 1: Place a quarter and a pencil on the table.

STEP 2: Pick up a quarter with your left hand, and hold it with your thumb and fingers in any way that feels natural and comfortable for you—but make sure you could show it to an audience if you wanted to (and if you had an audience).

STEP 3: Now, act like you need to pick the pencil up with your left hand. But you can't, can you? Ha! You've got a quarter in your left hand already.

What will you do?

Two choices: Either put the quarter down in your left palm so you can pick up the pencil with your fingertips, or transfer the coin to your right hand. Try it either way.

STEP 4: Try step 3 five times. Pause. Put the quarter down. Pick it up again with your left hand. Pretend to show it to the audience. Transfer the coin to your right hand so you can pick up the pencil with the left hand.

Okay. Aside from driving you crazy—which you know we like to do—why are we making you do this?

Easy.

So you can discover for yourself what feels like a natural way of moving a quarter from your left hand to your right. You probably moved the quarter with a combination of movements. This means that your right and left hands sort of came together a little. Your French drop should look and feel the same way—and the audience should never see it happen.

your big, important french Lesson

This is what sleight-of-hand magic is really all about. In any magic trick, study the real (not "fake") movement of your hands. Now make the "fake" move look the same. Your audience will not be able to tell the difference. There's a reason you have to move the quarter from one hand to the other—it has to be free to pick up the pencil. Look at how your hands look in a mirror. Do the sleight ten times or more in a row.

And be natural—don't get all goofy by twisting and turning your hands in ways that make you look like a spaz.

Now, let's turn our French lesson into a quick magic trick. Turn to the next page.

COiN extiNctiON #15

assigNmeNt: Make a coin disappear and reappear in your pant leg!

the frencH LessoN

If you've mastered the French drop (on pages 51–53), then you already know the secret to this move. Just keep practicing it. And practicing it. And, oh, yeah, practicing it.

magic must-Haves: Magic trunk

Homemade magic: A quarter, a pencil

Backstage

Nothing to do here, except maybe practice that French drop one more time. (Are you sensing a pattern here?) Then place the quarter and the pencil on the magic trunk.

sHow time!

"I have a thing for quarters."

STEP 1: Pick up the quarter with your left hand. Hold it (naturally) between your thumb and fingers.

"I like them because it's fun to do magic tricks with them."

STEP 2: Transfer the quarter to your right hand, using your own natural way of doing the French drop. The coin ends up at the base of the inside of your slightly curved left fingers. Your audience believes you've moved it to your right hand, which is now closed.

"But I can never seem to hold onto one."

STEP 3: Without stopping or hesitating, as soon as you (pretend) to move the coin to your right hand, reach for the pencil that is sitting nearby on the desk with your left hand. Pick up the pencil at one end, like you'd hold a magic wand.

"No matter what I do..."

STEP 4: Tap your closed right hand with the pencil.

"...no matter how hard I try..."

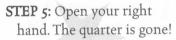

STEP 5: Open your right hand. The quarter is gone!

"...the quarter always gets away."

STEP 6: Put the pencil back down on the magic trunk. Reach down with your left hand to the inside of your left pant leg—just above your knee and a little bit to the back of your thigh.

"But if I look hard enough, I can find it again."

STEP 7: Hold the concealed quarter flat against the fabric of your pants with the fingers of your left hand. Your thumb should pinch the fabric on top of the quarter.

"Wait, I think I can feel it."

STEP 8: Pull the fabric of the pants very slightly away from your leg. You are now pinching the pants fabric and quarter together.

"Yes, I think it's here."

STEP 9: Use your right hand to help. Reach down with your right hand and kind of "wrap" a little bit of the pant fabric around the quarter. Your audience will see an "outline" of the coin through the fabric.

"This feels really weird!"

STEP 10: The right thumb and fingers hold the fabric close to the edge of the quarter. The left hand seems to pull the coin out of the "folds" of the fabric.

"Here it is!"

STEP II: Show the audience the quarter, and you're done!

HOMEWORK: You guessed it. You've already learned the French drop and know how to do it correctly by practicing in front of a mirror. Now you need to work on getting that quarter against your pant leg and make it seem like you're pulling it right from underneath your pants!

THE COIN KING

Musical magician Norm Neilsen has his own special spin on the *Miser's Dream*, a classic trick in which the magician pulls coins from the air. He uses a coin ladder, a small ladder along which the coins fall when the performer drops them onto it. Neilsen's prop emits musical tones as the coins roll along the rungs.

Poof!

assignment: Make a piece of paper and a pencil disappear!

Gone, Baby, Gone!

This is a classic misdirection, and a great extension of a trick you learned in *The Book of Illusions*. If you practice this trick like crazy, you'll have the audience staring at you slack-jawed, and it won't be because you've got something hanging out of your nose. The pencil is hiding behind your ear, and while you misdirect the audience to look at your ear, you hide the paper and then the pencil! Classic!

magic must-haves: Magic trunk

Homemade magic: A pencil (or pen), piece of paper (about 2 inches or 3 inches square), and a pair of pants with pockets (you should be wearing these)

> **Trick Tip:** You don't need to use a piece of paper with this trick. Use your imagination and try a small box, a coin, a sugar cube, even a ball. If you can slip it into your pocket undetected, you can use it in this trick!

Backstage

Don't you love tricks that don't have a lot of behind-the-scenes stuff to do? Us, too, and this is one of them! Just place the pencil and piece of paper on the magic trunk.

> **Trick Tip:** These instructions are for someone who writes with his or her right hand. If you're left-handed, you probably have a hard time using regular scissors. Fortunately, you don't need scissors for this trick. Just reverse everything, and do it left when we say right.

Show time!

"Pencils are tricky things."

STEP 1: Stand in front of the audience and face them. We know: They're not that pretty to look at—but they're all you've got! Pick up the piece of paper in your left hand and the pencil in your right.

"They love games and their favorite is hide-and-seek."

STEP 2: As you speak the above patter, you should slowly be turning your body sideways so that your left side is toward the audience. Hold the piece of paper in front of you with your left hand, just above waist high.

"Watch what I mean."

STEP 3: Hold the pencil with your right hand down by the pointy end. (If it's an unsharpened pencil, just put your fingers down where the pointy end would be.) Now, raise your right hand slightly, and "strike" the piece of paper with the pencil, just like a hammer hitting a nail. Most of the motion should be at your right elbow so that when you bend your right arm up, the eraser end of the pencil should come near your right ear. This is hugely important!

"One!"

STEP 4: Repeat step 3 exactly. Remember to bend at the elbow and bring the pencil end up so that it's near your right ear. When you bring the pencil down, strike the paper.

"Two!"

STEP 5: Here you go again: Bring your right arm back up to your ear, but this time you're doing something new. As you bend your right arm at the elbow, your right hand brings the pencil up to the level of your right ear. Carefully slip the pencil behind the top of your ear, and leave it there. Without stopping or pausing, bring your empty right hand down, and strike the paper with your right fingers. Remember, the movement of the empty hand during the third hit is exactly like the first two. Each hit is about one second long—not too fast.

"Three!"

STEP 6: Act very, very surprised that the pencil is gone. Stare at your right hand, wondering what could have happened to the pencil.

"What happened to the pencil?"

STEP 7: Pause a second or two as if you're thinking about where the pencil might be. Smile and slowly turn toward the audience until they can see your right side. Slowly point to the pencil with your right hand. Keep smiling, and now wink at the audience, because *you* know that *they* know where the pencil went. The audience will laugh!

"Crazy pencil."

STEP 8: Now it's your turn to laugh, at least on the inside. As your right hand points to the pencil, let your left hand drop down on your left side.

"It can't fool us."

STEP 9: Here's a tricky move that requires some misdirection. While your right side is toward the audience and everyone is looking at the pencil, the audience can't see your left side. Quietly, drop the piece of paper into your left pocket. Do this slowly without a lot of fumbling or movement. Don't worry about being caught. You have a lot of time to "get away" with this move.

"I told you pencils were tricky."

STEP 10: With your right hand, take the pencil out from behind your ear as you turn to the front. You should now be facing the audience. Bring your left hand up just like before, when it was holding the piece of paper. Act as if you are going to hit the paper, but:

"Hey! Wait a second! Now, where's the paper?"

STEP 11: Pause for a second or two.

"Oh, I know what you're thinking. I put it behind my ear over here, right?"

STEP 12: As you say this, turn your body slightly to the right again so the audience can see your left ear. And here's another great misdirection. Point to your left ear with your left hand. They'll all be looking at your ear to see if the paper's really there.

"Well, that's possible, I guess. Let's take a look."

STEP 13: While everyone looks at your left ear, slip the pencil into your right pocket. Start to turn toward the audience again.

"Oh, no! Not again!"

STEP 14: You are now facing your audience. Show them that both your hands are empty.

"Well, I was going to show you this trick with the paper and pencil, but it looks like both of them like to play hide-and-seek! Maybe next time!"

HOMEWORK: This is a trick that requires some smooth moves and turning your body so that the audience can't see your left side at certain times or your right side at others. Stand in front of a mirror and practice hiding the pencil and paper and turning away so you can't see where they've been hidden!

FISH BAIT AND SWITCH

Chung Ling Soo (1861–1918) was the stage name of William Robinson. Though not Asian, Robinson was so skilled with makeup that he created the character of the Asian magician Soo and toured the world, performing silently. One of the great appearance effects for which he is known is called Aerial Fishing. In this trick, which was probably invented in Asia, Soo cast a line from a fishing rod into the audience and made a fish appear on the hook. He then removed the fish and dropped it into a bowl so the audience, seeing it swim, could confirm that the fish was alive.

Today, you can see comedy magician Mac King perform this wonderful illusion at Harrah's Casino in Las Vegas. If you have the opportunity to see his daytime show, you'll be amazed as he recreates this classic routine and adds his own twist to it—he makes a fish disappear and reappear in his mouth!

textbook tipper #17

assignment: Make coins appear from a book!

the book nook

The great thing about a hardcover book is that when you open up the pages, you can see a little gap between the binding and the pages that runs the length of the spine. This is where your coins are really hiding!

magic must-haves: Magic trunk

homemade magic: A hardcover school textbook, ten to fifteen coins of different denominations

extras: One volunteer who doesn't know the trick

backstage

Open your hardcover book, and lay it flat. See the gap in the spine? That's the secret hiding place. Take five of your coins and place them in this gap. After the coins are placed, close the book.

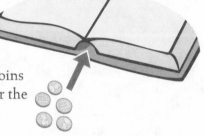

show time!

"Books cost a lot of money."

STEP 1: Put your closed book down on the magic trunk.

"But this is the first book that'll actually make money for me."

STEP 2: Open the book at the middle. Pick up your remaining coins (the ones you didn't hide in the gap). Let's say you have seven.

> **Trick Tip:** Try to find a book with a spine that is a little bit loose, so you can put coins inside it, but not so loose that the coins can fall out. You want to be able to carry the book without anyone hearing your hidden coins jingling!

"Here's what I'm talking about. Count with me: One, two, three, four, five, six, seven..."

STEP 3: Drop the coins into the middle of the pages from about one foot above the book, and as you drop each one, count it with the audience.

"Now, I need a volunteer."

STEP 4: Grab the book by its outside edges, and lift it off the table. (Keep the book flat while you lift it!)

"Hold out your hands. And when I drop the coins into them, I want you to squeeze your hands together tightly and hold them."

STEP 5: Tilt the book downward onto your volunteer's outstretched and cupped hands. Make sure that the spine of the book is open—you may have to open the book even wider by bending it backward just a little. The middle of the book should almost be resting on his hands. As you tilt the book, the coins hidden inside the spine will slide out, joining the others that are sliding off the pages. If you can do this pretty quickly, he'll never know that other coins are falling out of the spine.

"Now, hold these tightly."

STEP 6: After he squeezes his hands together and covers the coins, say:

"Remember, we started out with just the seven coins [or whatever the number of coins was]."

STEP 7: Wave your right hand over his hands.

"With a wave of my hand, I will add two coins to your pile."

STEP 8: Wave your left hand over his hands.

"Now, with another wave, I'll add another coin. Can you feel them getting heavier?"

STEP 9: He'll probably shake his head no.

"No? Well, let's try it again."

STEP 10: Wave both of your hands over his hands.

"I've just added two more coins. Now, I want you to slowly open your hands and count each coin out loud as you place them in my hand."

STEP 11: Sure enough, when he counts, he'll discover that he's got twelve coins—five more than he thought he had!

try it this way!

After your volunteer is holding all the coins, reach into your pocket, and pull out a small group of coins. Pretend to take one, and then pretend to throw it toward your volunteer's closed hand. Now when he opens his hands, it'll look like you made a coin travel from your hand to his.

then try it this way!

Are you a math whiz? Then next time, figure out backstage the total value of the coins hidden inside the book. Instead of using the number of coins in your patter, do the trick using the total value of the coins. Get your volunteer a little earlier—before step 2. When you count the coins onto the open book, have the volunteer add them up with you. For example, if you drop a dime and a nickel onto the open book, say, *"That's fifteen cents."* Drop a quarter onto the book and say, *"Now, that's forty cents."* And so on. Add the value of the hidden coins to the ones you totaled with your volunteer, and in step 10 have your volunteer shake his closed hands. Claim that you can determine the new value of the coins by the jingle. Then, add up the new total with your volunteer, and amaze your audience with your ability to add by sound!

HOMEWORK: Everything depends on being able to tilt the book at the correct angle so the coins fall out of their hiding place at the same time as the ones on the pages. Practice that until it's so smooth even *you* don't know how it happened!

PASS THE SALT!

Imagine shaking a little bit of salt into your hand, making your hand into a fist, and pouring some out. Now imagine that you are able to make the stream of salt practically endless as it pours and pours from your hand onto the floor. This crazy salt trick was invented by Roy Benson (1915–1978), but it was made into a miracle by Dutch magician Fred Kaps (1926–1980), who featured it in his silent act. Kaps, who in 1972 was called the "World's Greatest Magician," pretended to be "out of control" during his salt trick, when he couldn't stop the endless flow of salt from his hands. This bit of comedy added to the mystery, as no one knew where all the salt came from.

---

aiR caNdy

assignment: Make candy disappear by throwing it into the air!

Homemade magic: A bowl of candy

candy is dandy

This is one crazy trick, but it really works! You're only pretending to take candy from a bowl, but you're really taking—nothing! That's right, absolutely nothing! So when you're throwing the "candy" into the air, you're really throwing only air into the air!

> **Trick Tip:** This is a very quick magic trick. It happens very fast and it appears to happen at the spur of the moment, as if you just thought of it while finishing up a different trick. To make it natural, keep a bowl of M&M's (or similar candy) on the table while you're doing your whole act. You might want to eat a couple right before starting the trick.

backstage

Just make sure you've got that bowl of candy nearby and that you haven't eaten too much of it. (We know how you are with candy!)

show time!

"My mom doesn't like me to eat too much candy."

STEP 1: Reach in with your left hand and grab some candy. Pop a couple of pieces into your mouth and chew.

"She says it's bad for my teeth and it ruins my appetite for things like broccoli and peas."

STEP 2: Reach into the bowl and grab a few more candies with your left hand.

"But I told my mom not to worry."

STEP 3: With your right hand, reach into your left hand, and simply pretend to take one of them. Don't really take any—just fake it. This is called a mime.

"This is magic candy."

STEP 4: Blow on the fingertips of your right hand.

"I just add a little air."

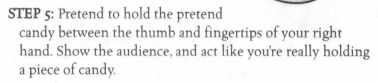

STEP 5: Pretend to hold the pretend candy between the thumb and fingertips of your right hand. Show the audience, and act like you're really holding a piece of candy.

"It turns invisible..."

STEP 6: Be sure to stare at your right hand as though you really are holding something in it as you put the candies that are in your left hand back into the bowl.

"...and the calories and the sugar are gone!"

STEP 7: Open your right hand fully. Show the audience that the cand in that hand has become "invisible"! Now, eat the "invisible" candy.

"Mmmm, that's really good. You should try one!"

NOW TRY IT THIS WAY!

Instead of eating the invisible candy yourself, call up someone from the audience. Place the "candy" in your right hand into her hand. Now act all surprised when you both discover that it's vanished!

OR TRY IT THIS WAY!

You're over at a friend's house, and you see a bowl of peanuts. Don't run over to it right away, but just wait until you can casually get near it. Then offer to show your pal how you can eat peanuts without gaining any calories. Reach into the tray and mime taking one peanut; don't let him see you're not really taking anything. Hold your hand just like you would if you really had a peanut. Take one step away from the bowl of nuts, and make a fist around your "peanut." Blow on your closed hand. Gradually open it to show your friend that the peanut has vanished.

anδ now with peanut butter

If you're in your own house and there's a jar of peanuts, sneak into your kitchen, take a very small bit of peanut butter, and put it on your palm. Then, when you pretend to squeeze the "peanut" with your fist, you open your hand to reveal that it turned into peanut butter, thanks to your super-strength!

anδ money, too!

This also works really well with a bunch of coins. Just take a handful of change and put it on a table or in a small bowl. Do the same trick, and show your friends how you can make money disappear! (Or better yet, use their money and don't give it back! Well, maybe that's not such a great idea if you want to keep your friends.)

HOMEWORK: The trick here is to convince the audience that you've taken a piece of candy when you haven't. Get some candy, and stand in front of a mirror, practicing the mime. You can also take a break and eat some candy for real!

FLY, FLY AWAY

In a dove act, the trick is to make lots and lots of live doves continually appear and disappear. Magicians who perform a dove act are referred to as *dove workers*. They make the doves appear and vanish without the use of boxes or cages. Silk handkerchiefs, scarves, newspapers, and playing cards are shown to be free from gimmickry as the birds magically appear at the performer's fingertips.

Abe Cantu came to the United States from Mexico in the 1940s and studied with Paul Fox, who had privately developed a dove act but had never shown it to an audience. Cantu may have been the first magician to perform it publicly. The novelty of making doves appear was an instant sensation, and making all kinds of birds appear and disappear is still a popular trick. Comedy magician Johnny Thompson not only makes doves appear, he also makes bird droppings appear on his tuxedo!

HANKY-PANKY #19

assignment: Make a coin disappear from under a handkerchief!

Homemade magic: A large handkerchief (the silk ones in your kit are too small, so don't use them) or bandanna, a quarter, a thin rubber band less than one inch long, and two hard-boiled eggs. (Okay, we're just kidding about the eggs, but we thought you might be hungry by now.)

extras: A volunteer who doesn't know the trick

Backstage

Place the rubber band around your fingers and thumb of your right hand. Place the hanky over your right hand so no one can see the rubber band.

Show time!

"I need a volunteer from the audience."

STEP 1: When your volunteer steps up, hand him the quarter, using your nonhanky hand.

"This is a special magic trick because you get to feel the magic."

STEP 2: Hold your right hand palm up, and extend your fingers like an upside-down octopus. (Okay, a five-legged octopus.) Push a bit of the handkerchief into your right hand, forming a small "well."

"Now, drop the quarter into the handkerchief."

STEP 3: Once the quarter's in the well, move the fingertips of your right hand together. This will let the rubber band slip off your fingertips and wrap around the coin in the hanky. The rubber band will hold the quarter in place.

STEP 4: Turn your hand that has the hanky in it over, and immediately grab the rubber band and the coin through the

67

handkerchief with your other hand. Be sure that you are hiding the rubber band.

"Now, I want you to feel the coin through the handkerchief."

STEP 5: As your volunteer's doing that, grab the corner of the handkerchief with your free hand.

"Can you feel the coin there? Good, because your sense of touch is about to play a trick on you. On the count of three, let go of the coin. One...two...three!"

STEP 6: As your volunteer releases the coin, give the hanky a little shake. The rubber band will hold the coin in place, but your audience will assume that the coin will fly free from the hanky. Keep the hanky moving, and they'll figure they missed seeing the coin fall. Look on the floor for the coin. It's gone!

"Fooled you!"

HOMEWORK: The rubber band is the tricky part. Practice the release in step 6 so that it seems smooth and natural.

Trick Tip: Remember, the audience will look where you look. Be sure to not look at the handkerchief, or they'll suspect that the coin might be hidden there. A good idea is to have another coin that looks just like yours hidden somewhere in the room or in a pocket. You can then show the volunteer where the coin went!

FISH BOWLING

In 1909, magician Han Ping Chien used the long Chinese robes he wore and some large scarves to make a stack of nine fishbowls, complete with water and fish, appear onstage in 1909. Nine years later, Jack Gwynne and Doc Nixon, two American magicians, created a device that would let magicians do the trick without having to wear the long robes.